ColourScene
Snapshot 2

THE
LAST YEAR OF
THE
RTs and RFs

N. J. Eadon-Clarke

DTS
Publishing

ISBN: 978-1-900515-37-5 © 2007 N. J. Eadon-Clark

Published by: DTS Publishing PO Box 105, Croydon CR9 2TL *www.dtspublishing.co.uk*

Printed by: Ian Allan Printing Limited

British Library Cataloguing in Publication Data. A catalogue record for this book is available from the British Librar

FRONT COVER: RT1928 TB at the country terminus of route 146 Downe village the home of the famous Charles Darwin. In June 19 it became a training bus at Bexleyheath and it was sold for scrap in May 1979. **4 March 1978**

FRONTISPIECE: Although no longer in service RTs could still be seen in Central London on training duties, here we have a classic London scen RT4650 the Riverside garage training bus crosses Westminster Bridge. In February 1979 it was sold to Wombwell. **21 October 1978**

BACK COVER – UPPER: Inside Kingston bus station and we find RF314 blinded for route 218 on the last day of scheduled RF operatic This RF like 471 pictured earlier had returned to service in November 19 77 following four years as a Reigate staff bus, it too went to Booth for scrap via BCA. **30 March 1979**

BACK COVER – LOWER: Inside Kingston bus station and we find RF314 blinded for route 218 on the last day of scheduled RF operatic This RF like 471 pictured earlier had returned to service in Nov 77 following four years as a Reigate staff bus, it too went to Booth's scrap via BCA. **30 March 1979**

FOREWORD

This book, the second in the 'ColourScene Snapshot' series, focuses on the last months of London's RT and RF buse in revenue earning service in the Capital.

RT1 entered passenger service in August 1939. The preliminary batch of 150 buses entered service between Janua 1940 and February 1942. Thereafter no further vehicles would be constructed until after the end of World War II. The first po war production vehicles entered service in 1947 when Weymann bodied RT402 did so from Leyton garage on Saturda 10th May and Park Royal bodied RT152 joined it at Leyton on 23rd May. The final deliveries were in 1954, but 144 vehicle were stored as being surplus to requirements and it would be August 1959 before the final RT entered service, by which tin new Routemasters were already being received,

The last RT in London Transport revenue earning service bowed out on 7 April 1979 as illustrated in this book.

The first twenty five RFs were built for private hire duties and thus differed from the rest by having glass in the coving the roof and being built to a length of 27ft 6ins. All other RFs were built to a length of 30 ft. The private hire vehicles entere passenger service between April 1951 and June 1951. The others did so between October 1951 and March 1954.

The last RF in London Transport revenue earning serviced bowed out on 30 March 1979 as illustrated in this book.

I wish to thank Mike Davis of DTS Publishing for all his advice including the scanning and layout of all the content produce the finished article. Thanks are also due to Keith Hamer and Maurice Bateman for reading the captions (albeit witho seeing the accompanying photographs), making corrections and adding information about disposal dates and subseque histories. Any remaining errors are mine. I hope the photographs in this book capture the mood of the final months and la days in service of these two classic London vehicles.

All photographs by the author

Nigel Eadon-Clarke   November 200
Chislehurst
Kent
UK

INTRODUCTION

All 4,825 RTs were mounted on AEC Regent III chassis. Post war bodywork to a width of 7 feet 6 inches was provided Park Royal Vehicles, Weymann, Saunders and Cravens. Similar bodywork was also provided by Park Royal Vehicles, etro-Cammell and Weymann on Leyland Titan chassis which resulted in 1,631 RTLs, whilst the 500 eight feet wide RTWs ere bodied by Leyland themselves. During the 1950s and 1960s and as stated on the poster carried by the last vehicles Barking and illustrated in this book London Transport could boast the largest standardised bus fleet in the world and the ulk of the single deckers and double deckers were members of the RT and RF family. Several times in the 1960s and 970s plans had been made to replace the RTs, partly by Routemasters and partly by newer types such as the Daimler eetline. However the robustness and reliability of the RT design was such that they would often cover for a shortage of outemasters and the unreliable newer types in the 1970s. Thus RTs survived in service for 40 years which is an xceptional achievement only recently eclipsed by its successor, the Routemaster. However it must be noted that the vast ajority of the remaining Routemasters were substantially rebuilt and re-powered with modern-day non-AEC engines hereas RTs continued to the end unaltered. Route 94 was one of the routes that had a very long association with RTs eing home to the type from around 1950 until August 1978. Towards the end many RTs looked shabby having been tained longer than expected although the best examples (those recently re-certified) naturally found their way to Barking other garages received replacement types.

All 700 RFs were mounted on AEC Regal Mk IV chassis and bodywork to a width of 7 feet 6 inches was provided by etro-Cammell. 225 examples were ordered for the red central bus fleet and were delivered without entrance doors. Later onversions to one person operation required the fitting of power operated doors. Kingston will always be associated with e RF type the first examples being seen there on route 213 from Norbiton and Sutton garages in December 1952. ithdrawal of the central area examples in substantial numbers began in Spring 1976 and most had been replaced within he year, but due to the problems of space within Kingston garage precluding the installation of longer inspection pits quired for newer vehicles with a larger internal capacity it was decided to re-certify 25 vehicles for potential operation for further three years. In consequence many of these received the new LT roundel in place of the traditional gold fleetname d many had other detail differences in livery application.

I have deliberately included several photos on the 'last days' to try and capture the atmosphere on the last day

arage codes used in this book:

AD – Palmers Green	BX – Bexleyheath	HW – Southall	TB – Bromley
AM – Plumstead	HD – Harrow Weald	K – Kingston	TL – Catford
BK – Barking		S – Shepherd's Bush	

ast scheduled days of RT or RF normal operation of the routes featured in this book

oute	Garage	Date	Replacement type the following day
1	AD	3 March 1978	Daily converted to RM
4	TL	21 April 1978	Daily converted to DMS
9	BX	21 April 1978	Daily converted to DMS
2	TL	21 April 1978	Saturday allocation converted to RM
22	AM	21 April 1978	Daily converted to RM
6	TB	21 April 1978	Daily converted to BL
05	HW & S	29 April 1978	Daily converted to RM
95	BK	25 May 1978	Daily converted to crew DMS
98	BK	25 May 1978	Daily converted to crew DMS
0	HD	14 July 1978	Daily converted to RM
4	TL	25 August 1978	Daily converted to RM
7	TB & TL	26 August 1978	Mon – Fri cross linked RTs replaced by RMs
2	TB	26 August 1978	Daily converted to RM
7	BK	27 October 1978	Daily converted to RM, one Saturday RT working retained
18 & 219	K	30 March 1979	Daily converted to LS from Norbiton garage
2	BK	7 April 1979	Daily converted to RM

ABOVE: RT1831 BK on route 62 at Becontree Station. In December 1978 this would be sold to a buyer in Belgium. **26 February 197**

BELOW: RT3286 BK on route 62 at Chadwell Heath. This bus would be withdrawn from service in April 1978 and is pictured thus in Barki garage yard later in this book. It was sold to Wombwell in December 1978. **26 February 1978**

ABOVE: RT3202 TB was one of the RTs returned from LCBS in September 1972 it is seen on route 146 at Keston Common at the junction of Westerham Road and Heathfield Road. In June 1978 it became a training bus at Sutton. It was withdrawn in January 1979 and sold to Wombwell in February 1979. **4 March 1978**

BELOW: RT2345 AM seen in Adelaide Avenue outside Hilly Fields on route 122. It would be removed from service the following month and sold to a buyer in West Germany in May 1979. **4 March 1978**

ABOVE: RT4190 TB seen at the terminus of route 94, Petts Wood station, the railway line is behind and the corrugated iron sheeting wa erected after the demolition of an adjacent cinema. It remained at Bromley garage until RT operation ceased at TB and is pictured later this book after withdrawal. **4 March 1978**

BELOW: RT1677 BX in Rennell Street Lewisham before the construction of the new Lewisham shopping centre. It lays over at the termina point of route 89. The following month it became a training bus at Mortlake and was withdrawn in January 1979. Initially preserved, it wa exported to Spain for promotional use. **5 March 1978**

ABOVE: Returned to revenue earning service the previous month, RT4641BX heading for Lewisham alongside Blackheath Pond in Prince of Wales Road on route 89. It didn't stay in service for long and moved to become a training bus at Loughton garage the following month upon the cessation of RT operation at BX, it was withdrawn and sold to Wombwell in January 1979. **5 March 1978**

BELOW: RT3251 BX working on route 89 has just completed the long drag up Shooters Hill which is a stern test for any fully laden bus. The following month after RT operation at BX ended it received some attention at Croydon garage and then moved to BK in May 1978 remaining until the end and taking part in the final cavalcade. **5 March 1978**

ABOVE: Bexleyheath garage which still exists largely unchanged today is unique as being the only garage built new for trolleybuses. Standing outside are three buses none of which are garaged at BX. Two Plumstead based RTs at the terminus of route 122. RTs 686 and 745 stand either side of a Sidcup Routemaster on route 229. RT745 was scrapped the following month, but RT 686 moved to Bromley garage for a couple more months of revenue earning service, then stored and later became a training bus at Catford before being sold for scrap in December 1979. **5 March 1978**

BELOW: Sun streams through the roof panels onto Bexleyheath RT3094 which heads a line of RTs surrounded by B20 type Daimler Fleetlines which work on route 96. The RT was withdrawn on 15 April and sent to Wombwell a fortnight later. **5 March 1978**

BOVE: RT2250 BX swings around Blendon roundabout Bexley on route 89 heading for Eltham. This RT was withdrawn the following onth when RT services finished at Bexleyheath and after some months in store was sold Mercedes Benz at Hayes, Middlesex in December 978 and exported to Germany. **11 March 1978**

ELOW: RT1619 BX seen on route 89 in Bexley village, it carries side advertisements for Allders Department store in Eltham which has ng since closed. This bus was stored for a while after withdrawal at the end of RT operation at BX, but eventually sold for scrap in December 978. **11 March 1978**

ABOVE: On a grey March day in Bexley village RT3408 BX works route 89. This RT was stored the following month and then moved to Barking in September 1978 where it worked the last scheduled Mon-Fri working on route 87 the following month; it is pictured later in this book. **11 March 1978**

BELOW: Slade Green railway station is the setting for this view of RT4195 AM on route 122, It briefly operated at Bexleyheath the following month before moving to Barking, it was withdrawn in July 1978 and sold for scrap in August 1978. **11 March 1978**

ABOVE: A short working on route 122 sees RT2293 AM at Brockley Rise. After the end of RT service at Plumstead it moved to Barking. It was withdrawn and sold in November 1978 and still exists today with a preservationist. **11 March 1978**

BELOW: Also at Brockley Rise we find RT3750 TB at the terminus of route 94. This bus would perform the last journey on route 146 as shown later in this book. **11 March 1978**

LEFT: The Crystal Palace television and radio mast forms the backdrop to two RTs awaiting their next journeys on route 122. The vehicles are RTs 686 and 714 both from Plumstead garage. RT714 moved to Bromley for their final months of operation and then in August 1978 it returned to Plumstead as a training bus. In November 1979 it was exported to Canada. As noted earlier, RT686 moved to bromley and then to Catford as a training bus before being sold for scrap in December 1979. **12 March 1978**

BELOW: The classic design lines of an RT are illustrated here by RT714 AM waiting to depart from Crystal Palace on route 122. **12 March 1978**

ABOVE: Eltham Well Hall Road is the setting for RT3410 AM working on route 122. Following the end of RT operations at Plumstead in April it moved to Barking. In October 1978 it became a training bus at Loughton and sold for scrap one month later. **12 March 1978**

BELOW: RT397 AM is seen on route 122 in Green's End Woolwich. The next month it moved to Bromley and on to Barking in August 1978. In October 1978 it became a training bus at Alperton before being sold to Wombwell in July 1979. **12 March 1978**

13

ABOVE: RT3342 AD seen in a snowstorm in Potter's Road, New Barnet while working route 261, this was one of the last RTs workir from Palmers Green garage and left for further service at Barking this very evening. It was withdrawn in August 1978 and sold for scra **17 March 1978**

BELOW: A shabby RT1744 a training bus based at Potters Bar garage waits outside New Barnet railway station. It was withdrawn tv months later and sold to Wombwell in August 1978. **17 March 1978**

ABOVE: RT2258 HD is working on route 140 and is seen here at Queensbury station. It was withdrawn and sold to Wombwell in June 1978. **17 March 1978**

BELOW: Seen earlier working from Plumstead; Baston Road, Hayes is the setting for RT397 TB working on route 146 heading for Keston and Downe. **18 March 1978**

ABOVE: The George public house in Hayes is the backdrop for this view of RT785 TB on route 146. This bus lasted in service only unti the following month and was sold for scrap in May 1978. **18 March 1978**

BELOW: Lee railway station is visible behind RT2410 TL working route 94, it would be unlicensed later this month and became a trainin bus at Walworth before sale to Wombwell in April 1979. **18 March 1978**

ABOVE: During its last few days in service RT3513 TL in Beckenham High Street working route 54 heading for Woolwich. It was sold to Wombwell later this month. **23 March 1978**

BELOW: The non under-lined fleetname is clearly visible in this view of RT4803 TL on route 54 at Elmers End Green. In June 1978 it became a training bus at Camberwell and was sold to Wombwell in March 1979. **23 March 1978**

ABOVE: Heading to Croydon is RT4448 TL in Addiscombe Road on route 54. In June 1978 it became a training bus at Stonebridge and was withdrawn and sold to Wombwell in January 1979. **23 March 1978**

BELOW: Standing opposite The Fox public house in Keston used as a peak hour short working terminus of route 146 we find RT397 TB. **23 March 1978**

ABOVE: RT4181 BK had been recently transferred from Palmers Green garage and would stay in service at Barking until the end. It is captured working on route 62 outside Barking station. After its revenue earning service ended it moved to Hendon as a training bus before being sold to Wombwell in March 1979. **24 March 1978**

BELOW: Another RT bought back from LCBS in September 19 72, RT4515 BK in Valence Avenue Becontree at its junction with Wood lane on its way back to Barking on route 62. It too stayed at Barking until the end following which it became a training bus at Highgate (Holloway) garage before sale to Wombwell in February 1979. **24 March 1978**

ABOVE: Upney station is the location of this view of RT2212 BK on route 62. After a short spell as a training bus at Hendon it was sold to Wombwell in September 1978. **24 March 1978**

BELOW: Until the previous month this RT had been the Cricklewood staff bus, but such was the shortage of serviceable RTs it was pressed into service for just one month. A proud crew pose in front of RT233 HD at the Mill Hill terminus of route 140. The following month it was sold for scrap. **26 March 1978**

ABOVE: RT669 HD takes on passengers while working on route 140 in Honeypot Lane, Queensbury Circle. This bus was withdrawn in April and sold to Wombwell in June 1978. **26 March 1978**

BELOW: Shaftesbury Avenue Harrow sees RT848 HD at work on route 140. After its revenue earning service ended it spent a brief spell as a training bus at Fulwell, but from October 1978 it became the 'turnover' bus nominally allocated to Camberwell to allow trainees to learn how to right a bus that had fallen over. It was sold to Wombwell in April 1981. **26 March 1978**

ABOVE: Leaving Heathrow Airport is RT3220 HD on route 140. After route 140 was converted to RM in July it moved to Bromley for thei last month of service after which it became the Dalston training bus before being sold and ultimately exported to Spain. **26 March 1978**

BELOW: About to be passed by a Metropolitan near Lewisham Odeon cinema is Bexleyheath based RT3408 on route 89. After a spel unlicensed following the end of RT in revenue earning service at Bexleyheath it returned to service at Barking in September 1978, but only for one month before transfer to become a training bus at Barking and sold to Wombwell in May 1979. **27 March 1978**

ABOVE: During its last few days in ownership RT3094 BX is seen on route 89 outside St. Margarets Church Blackheath. It was sold at the end of this month to Wombwell. **27 March 1978**

BELOW: RT2250 BX on route 89 in Eltham High Street. **1 April 1978**

ABOVE: RF337 is a vehicle that always operated with a conductor hence the lack of power operated front doors. It is seen here at Cobham during their annual open day owned by the Chiltern Omnibus Group and was for sale for continued preservation. **2 April 1978**

BELOW: Preserved Saunders bodied RT1320 working the free connecting bus service at Weybridge station during the LBPG's annual open day, the next day it would be loaned back to LT for use as a training bus at Camberwell garage to cover a critical shortage in LT's own training fleet. **2 April 1978**

ABOVE: Heading for Crystal Palace on route 122 is RT1777 AM seen here at Bexleyheath railway station. Later this month it became a training bus at Clapton; withdrawn and sold in April 1979, it is currently stored for preservation. **9 April 1978**

BELOW: An East Kent Plaxton bodied coach in 'National' livery passes RT3949 BX which arrived from Southall the previous month works on route 89 in Shooters Hill Road Blackheath. Later this month it became a training bus at Fulwell and was sold to Wombwell in March 1979. **4 April 1978**

ABOVE: Outside Shooters Hill Police Station we find RT379 AM on route 122. Later this month it moved to Bromley and following the end of their RT operation it moved to Barking in August 1978 where it stayed until the end. It then became a training bus at Alperton before being sold to Wombwell in July 1979. **9 April 1978**

BELOW: RT1107 AM seen at Ladywell on route 122. This is another RT that moved to Bromley later this month, it then became a Camberwell training bus until withdrawal in August 1978 and sale to a private owner. **9 April 1978**

ABOVE: Woolwich General Gordon Place is one terminus of route 54 and here we see RT1152 TL waiting to depart to Croydon. It was withdrawn ten days later and it would be sold to Wombwell in June 1978. **10 April 1978**

BELOW: Plumstead training bus RT4630 is seen here being used to give instruction at Woolwich Artillery Place. Withdrawn in January 1979 and sold to Wombwell in February 1979. **10 April 1978**

ABOVE: RT2047 TL on route 54 in Woolwich outside the Kings Arms public house opposite Woolwich garrison. In June 1978 it became a training bus at Walworth and was withdrawn and sold to Wombwell in July 1978. **10 April 1978**

BELOW: RT4803 TL seen at one terminus of route 54 Woolwich General Gordon place with its blind display set for its return journey to Croydon. **10 April 1978**

ABOVE: Seen approaching Eltham at Avery Hill is RT1791 BX while working on route 89. It moved to Barking later this month and stayed to the end before becoming an Aldenham works staff bus. It was sold for scrap in March 1979. **15 April 1978**

BELOW: RT1538 TB approaches Farthing Street heading for Downe village on route 146. It was sold the following month to Wombwell. **15 April 1978**

ABOVE: Also sold to Wombwell the following month, RT785 TB waits outside Downe church ready to depart from Downe village on route 146. **15 April 1978**

BELOW: Withdrawn RT4642 awaits collection for scrap by Wombwell at the rear of Bexleyheath garage, having been withdrawn on 9 March. **16 April 1978**

ABOVE: Emerging from Plumstead garage onto Wickham Lane is RT1107 AM about to take up duties on route 122. **16 April 1978**

BELOW: Seen in Plumstead High Street opposite Lakedale Road is RT3997 AM on route 122. It was sold to Wombwell the following month. **16 April 1978**

ABOVE: A relatively empty Westhorne Avenue Eltham sees RT4126 TL on route 122 being overtaken by a mini. Later this month it move to Barking and then became a training bus at Bow before withdrawal and sale to Wombwell in December 1978. **16 April 1978**

BELOW: Seen in Eltham Road passing the junction of Kidbrooke Park Road is RT3410 AM on route 122. After RT revenue earning servic ended at Plumstead later this month it moved to Barking for further service. In October 1978 it became a training bus at Loughton and wa sold to Wombwell in November 1978. **16 April 1978**

ABOVE: RT1107 AM seen earlier leaving Plumstead garage is now in Forest Hill on route 122 passing the Railway Telegraph public house. **16 April 1978**

BELOW: Waiting to turn out of Dartmouth Road Forest Hill into Kirkdale while on route 122 is RT1654 AM. It moved to Barking after RT operation ended at Plumstead later this month, but didn't last until the end, instead it was withdrawn in March 1979 and sold to Wombwell April 1979. **16 April 1978**

ABOVE: These four RTs are lined up alongside Bromley garage, RT4190 is at the front and behind it are RTs: 1538 and 785 and bringing up the rear is RT397. RTs 1538 and 4190 both passed to Wombwell, but RT4190 was rescued by members of the Barking garage staff and social club. **16 April 1978**

BELOW: Croydon Fairfield Halls is one terminus of route 54 and here stands RT3871 TL awaiting its return trip to Woolwich. Following the end of RT operation at Catford it moved to Bow as a training bus and still exists today in the fleet of London Bus Company Heritage fleet. **17 April 1978**

ABOVE: An empty road at Bellingham sees RT840 TL working on route 54. After the end of RT operation at Catford it became a training bus at Hornchurch. It was withdrawn and sold to Wombwell in January 1979. **17 April 1978**

BELOW: RT2506 TL seen on route 94 in Rushey Green Catford. In May 1978 it became a training bus at Brixton and was sold for scrap March 1979. **17 April 1978**

ABOVE: Seen in Charlton on route 54 is RT4625 TL. It was withdrawn five days later and sold to Wombwell in June 1978. **17 April 197**

BELOW: Since 1977 this was the lowest numbered RT in the LT fleet, RT206 TL seen in John Wilson Street leaving Woolwich town cent▮ on route 54. Later this month it moved to Harrow Weald and is seen there later in this book, in May 1978 it became a training bus at Hendo▮ before sale to Wombwell in December 1978. **17 April 1978**

ABOVE: The last day of RT operation on route 146 sees RT3750 TB speeding past Downe Riding School. It carries a notice on its radiator explaining this sad fact. Following the end of RT revenue earning operation in August it became a training bus at Dalston before withdrawal in January 1979 and sale to Wombwell in February 1979. **21 April 1978**

RIGHT: RT3750 TB at the Bromley North terminus of route 146 on the last day of RT operation. **21 April 1978**

ABOVE: RT3750 TB at Bromley Nor[th] on the last day of RT operation of rou[te] 146, behind can be seen a LCBS AF class Fleetline on route 410 followe[d] by a Routemaster and Leylan[d] National. **21 April 1978**

LEFT: The time is 2152, the place [is] Downe village and the vehicle is th[e] 'last' RT on route 146 *i.e.* RT3750 T[B] **21 April 1978**

ABOVE: Waiting to depart from Downe on the very last RT journey on route 146 is RT3750 TB. As can be seen the lower deck is packed with enthusiasts and streamers. **21 April 1978**

BELOW: RT3750 TB arrives at Bromley garage having just completed the very last RT journey on route 146. Delays en route for photography means that the time now is 0010 so it actually operated for the last time on 22 April 1978. **22 April 1978**

ABOVE: The 21 April was also the la[st] day of RT operation on routes 89 fro[m] Bexleyheath garage, route 122 fro[m] Plumstead garage and route 54 fro[m] Catford garage. Here at 0035 on 22 Ap[ril] at BX garage is one of the last RTs [on] route 89: RT4712. This bus was r[e]tained by LT for operation at speci[al] events and still exists today as part [of] the museum collection, current[ly] painted in a 'gold' livery which it a[c]quired for the Queen's Golden Jubile[e] celebrations. **22 April 1978**

LEFT: Inside Plumstead garage ju[st] after the last RT on route 122 ha[s] completed its journey. RT4566 is see[n] at 0055 waiting the removal of i[ts] destination blinds. It was immediate[ly] de-licensed and moved to Sidcup ga[rage] for storage when formally with[drawn] in June 1978. Nevertheless [it] returned to use as a training bus an[d] was destined to be the last license[d] training RT in LT ownership remainin[g] in stock until sale to Wombwell in Ap[ril] 1980. **23 April 1978**

ABOVE: Two RTs stand at the Heathrow Airport bus station on route 140. RT3911 HD leads RT280 HD awaiting their departure times. RT3911 ill carries masking on its intermediate blind box following its previous use covering for a Routemaster at Holloway (an RM has a smaller ind). After the end of RT operation at HD it moved to Barking for further service until the end. It then became a training bus at Dalston until ale in June 1979. Between 1985 and 1999 it was preserved, but was then converted into a mobile burger bus and disappeared around 001. **23 April 1978**

BELOW: Rear view of RT280 HD and RT3911 HD on route 140 at Heathrow Airport bus station. RT280 had arrived from Catford earlier is month and returned back to Catford when route 140 was converted to RM in July although it was withdrawn and sold to Wombwell August when RT operation ended at Catford. **23 April 1978**

ABOVE: RT1171 HD inside the Heathrow Airport complex approaches the bus station on route 140. This bus was withdrawn an sold to Wombwell in June. **23 April 1978**

BELOW: The other RT route to reach Heathrow Airport is route 105, here RT4189 HW awaits departure just one week before th route would become operated by Routemasters. It would then move to Bexleyheath as a training bus, it is currently active in Ne Zealand. **23 April 1978**

ABOVE: The last week of RT operation on route 105 and RT4721 HW passes through Cranfield on the outskirts of Heathrow. This bus then spent a few weeks as a training bus at Finchley, but was sold to Wombwell in May 1978. **23 April 1978**

BELOW: RT4794 HW seen on route 105 in North Road Southall one week before the RTs would give way to Routemasters from both Southall and Shepherd's Bush garages. It then moved to Plumstead as a training bus until sold to Wombwell in August 1978. Of particular note is that this bus carries the last stock number delivered to LT on 11 November 1954. **23 April 1978**

ABOVE and BELOW: While the LT collection of preserved vehicles was housed at Syon Park RT3489 was parked outside for use b[y] school children to eat their packed lunches. The bus retains its Hounslow garage destination blinds for route 120 from Southall garage whic[h] lost its RTs on 28 January 1978 when the route received DMS type Daimler Fleetlines. **23 April 1978**

ABOVE: View from above, RT2566 HW passes under Greenford railway bridge while working on route 105. On the last day of April it became a training bus at Bexleyheath, but was withdrawn four weeks later, being exported to France in August 1978. **23 April 1978**

BELOW: Two Night routes still retained RTs in April, the N95 and N98 from Barking. RT operation on these routes would cease on 26/7 May when DMSs would take over. One month earlier RT3342 BK stands at Trafalgar Square on route N98 about to depart on the 0552 journey. Earlier in this book we saw this bus operating at Palmers Green, it was sold to Wombwell in August 1978. **29 April 1978**

ABOVE: Trafalgar Square at 0555 at the front is RT3342 BK about to depart and behind is RT1658 BK which will undertake the 0602 journey both on route N98. RT1658 stayed in service until October 1978 and then became a training bus at Romford. It still exists in store with the London Bus Company. **29 April 1978**

BELOW: Bloomsbury Red Lion Square sees RT678 BK waiting to depart on the 0610 journey on route N95. In October 1978 it would be sold to Wombwell. **29 April 1978**

ABOVE: This bus arrived from Plumstead after the end of RT operation at Plumstead. RT4037 BK passes the Daily Mirror building (since demolished) on route N95 in Fleet Street at 0629. In June 1978 it had a brief spell as a training bus at Upton Park although unlicensed in July it was resurrected in February 1979 to become a training bus at Potters Bar. After sale it was converted to open top and taken by its English owner to Majorca where its use was not permitted by the local authorities. They subsequently returned it to the UK and the RT saw service on Guernsey and was later exported to Denmark. **29 April 1978**

BELOW: Still in use RT1654 blinded for route 87 looks over at a line of withdrawn RTs in the yard of Barking garage at 0705, those identifiable from left to right are RTs: 3407, 3894, 3286 and 1561. This bus had also arrived from Plumstead a few days earlier, it was withdrawn in March 1979 and sold to Wombwell the following month. **29 April 1978**

47

ABOVE: RT1797 BK pauses outside Barking garage on route 87 at 0710. The following month it became a training bus at Barking and would be withdrawn and sold to Wombwell in August 1978. **29 April 1978**

BELOW: It is 0724 outside Barking garage and RT4037 BK arrives after completing its journey on route N95 this was the last night bus journey each night to return to the garage. **29 April 1978**

ABOVE: Northolt Rectory Parade sees RT206 HD on route 140. It can be seen that it displays a side blind in the front 'via' box. This RT is pictured earlier in this book working from Catford. **30 April 1978**

BELOW: With very little traffic to hinder it, RT4772 HD works on route 140 in South Harrow. This RT survives today with Abegweit Sightseeing Tours in Charlottetown, on Prince Edward Island, Canada in excellent condition. **30 April 1978**

ABOVE: The rear of RT3220 HD showing the yellow final destination display on route 140 while in service at Queensbury North Parade. The yellow blind indicates that this is one of two Sunday afternoon journeys diverted to serve Cherry Lane Cemetery. After route 140 lost its RTs it moved to Bromley and it then passed to Dalston as a training bus in August 1978 before being ultimately exported to Spain. **30 April 1978**

BELOW: Mill Hill railway bridge sees RT4711 HD on route 140. It was withdrawn and sold to Wombwell in June 1978. **30 April 1978**

ABOVE: Route 94 had a peak hour extension to Sidcup Alma Road. At that location we find RT714 TB. This RT also joined the Abegweit fleet on Prince Edward Island, Canada. **19 May 1978**

BELOW: A familiar sight around SE London at this time was 'Basil the Bus' the former RT4782 now owned for promotional use by the DIY and decorating chain 'FADS'. Here is passes down Bromley High Street. It later operated in Crewe before returning to Kent and sold again in 1988. It subsequently lost its body and was used as a glider winch in Norfolk, later being rebodied as a single deck caravan although it is not known if this work was ever completed. **20 May 1978**

ABOVE: Bromley garage continued to put their RTs on some unscheduled workings on routes normally the home the Routemasters. Here RT4356 TB makes such a journey on route 119A. It was withdrawn and sold to Wombwell in June 1978. **20 May 1978**

BELOW LEFT: Route 94 was worked by both Bromley and Catford garages. RT786 TB is seen at Lewisham bus station Route 94 should be solely operated by RMs at weekends. This RT is still in use with Imperial Buses in Essex. **3 June 1978**

BELOW RIGHT: The Sidcup garage training bus RT2992 at work on driver training duty in Sidcup Hill. It was withdrawn in August and sold to Wombwell in September 1978. **23 June 1978**

LEFT: The 'Magnificent 7' stunt team acquired former RF415 and it was usually to be found as here in Lee railway station approach. It was sold again in October 1980 and scrapped in 1991. **23 June 1978**

BELOW: Another unscheduled working on Routemaster route 119 sees RT714 TB in Bourne Way Hayes. **23 June 1978**

BOTTOM: One week later and RT714 TB is undertaking another Saturday working, this time on route 94 in Bromley High Street. **1 July 1978**

ABOVE: Another route 94 working on a Saturday sees RT3750 TB in Bromley High Street. **1 July 1978**

BELOW: The Weymouth annual bus rally and here is former RTL1174 in the livery of A & C McLennan. In 1988 it was sold out of preservation and exported to Germany. It later became open top promotional bus and still survives in 2007 in good running order. **2 July 1978**

TOP: RT2192 BK approaches Rainham on route 87. This RT was withdrawn in November 1978 and exported to Canada in March 1979 where it still exists today. **9 July 1978**

ABOVE: Rainham war memorial and RT3342 BK is working route 87. It was sold to Wombwell in August 1978. **9 July 1978**

LEFT: 'Bertie the Burger Bus' former RT3960 seen at work at the Lambeth Country Show. This bus disappeared off the scene for many years only to reappear as a mobile home at the Glastonbury music festival a few years ago. It has been 'shrunk' in height to 4 metres suggesting that it either lives abroad or travels extensively outside the UK. **23 July 1978**

ABOVE: RT379 TB working on route 47 at Farnborough Nile Cottages. Seen earlier in this book operating from Plumstead it would also operate from Barking from August 1978 until October 1978 and then become a training bus at Alperton before sale to Wombwell in July 1979. **28 July 1978**

BELOW: Croydon 'The Eagle' and RT1850 TB works route 119 which was scheduled for RMs. When RT operation finished at Bromley in August this bus became a training bus at Bexleyheath until its sale to Wombwell in April 1979. **28 July 1978**

ABOVE: RT3351 TL on route 94 at Grove Park. After RT operation ended at Catford in August this bus moved to Bow as a training bus. It was sold to Wombwell in February 1980 and is pictured there at the end of this book. **8 July 1978**

BELOW: RT3871 TL on route 94 at Grove Park. This bus was sold to a private owner in April 1979 and still exists today as part of the London Bus Company heritage fleet. **28 July 1978**

LEFT: With **a** Routemaster side blind in the front and route '61' showing in the canopy box RT2602 TB works route 94 at Petts Wood. The following month it was sold to Wombwell. **28 July 1978**

BELOW: Climbing past Orpington railway station heading for Lewisham is RT3467 TL on route 94. This RT had arrived from Harrow Weald earlier in the month and would pass to Barking next month. It would remain in service until October 1978 and then become a training bus at Wood Green before sale to Wombwell in March 1979. **28 July 1978**

BOTTOM: Also received from Harrow Weald we see RT280 TL. It is seen here running off service to Bromley Garage in a part of Bromley High Street now pedestrianised. It was withdrawn and sold to Wombwell the following month. **29 July 1978**

ABOVE: Bromley Market Square and a part that is also now shut to traffic and RT1850 TB pulls away from the bus stop outside Heals department store now long since closed. **5 August 1978**

BELOW: RT379 TB arrives at Brockley Rise while working on route 94 before its move to Barking later this month. **5 August 1978**

ABOVE: RT2623 TB seen at the Greenway Orpington on route 94. After the end of RT operation at Bromley it became a training bus at Sidcup and in July 1979 it was one of several RTs bought by the Giraffe Bus Company in Lusaka Zambia **11 August 1978**

LEFT: Petts Wood High Street is the location for this view of RT1790 TB on route 94. **11 August 1978**

BELOW: Route 94 had a peak hour extension to Sidcup station. RT1599 TB stands in Cray Avenue, Sidcup. This bus had been refurbished for the Queens Silver Jubilee parade in 1977 and had once been expected to be the last RT in service (when Harrow Weald was expected to be the last home of RTs). After operation at Bromley it became a training bus at Bexleyheath until March 1979. It was sold in July 1979 and is currently preserved. **11 August 1978**

ABOVE: With blinds set for the return journey to Lewisham RT2541 TL stands at the peak hour terminus of route 94, Alma Road Sidcup. It subsequently moved to Barking and lasted until the end taking part in the final cavalcade. It then was withdrawn and sold to Wombwell in June 1979 and subsequently exported to Double Deck Tours at Niagara Falls in Canada. **11 August 1978**

BELOW: This location in Sidcup High Street is just outside the Driving Test Centre. RT651 TL had arrived from Harrow Weald garage in July 1978 and is returning from Sidcup station on route 94. When RT operation at Catford finished it moved to become a training bus at Hornchurch before sale to Wombwell in February 1979. **11 August 1978**

ABOVE: This location in Bromley is known locally as 'Clarks College' which is where Masons Hill meets Homesdale Road, RT4210 TL crosses the junction on route 94. It moved later in the month to become a training bus at Kingston. After sale it operated as the yellow Holste Beers bus between 1979 and 1986. **11 August 1978**

BELOW: RT2143 TB stands in Baring Road, Grove Park heading for Lewisham on route 94. After its revenue earning service finishe with the end of RT operation at Bromley this bus become a 'skid bus' at the Chiswick works training school before export to Japan **11 August 1978**

LEFT: Standing in the grounds of the East Anglian Transport Museum near Lowestoft is preserved RF503. It had entered preservation in February 1977 and remains as such today. **13 August 1978**

LEFT: These two former LT RFs: 371 & 527 are in use as staff transport by Howard Rotavators of Halesworth, Suffolk. They are seen at their factory between journeys, both were withdrawn and sold by the end of 1978. **18 August 1978**

BELOW: The yard of Mulley's Motorways at Ixworth Suffolk was well known for a collection of withdrawn vehicles. Here former RT4439 awaits its fate having been removed from service the previous year. It was scrapped some time after 1979. **22 August 1978**

63

ABOVE: The last Friday of Catford garage's operation on route 94 and RT1301 TL speeds along Lee High Road. It then moved to Barking for further service lasting until the end where upon it was withdrawn and exported to the USA. **25 August 1978**

BELOW: At the same spot RT422 TL works route 94. This bus would later this day be the last scheduled RT into Catford garage and carries suitable decoration for this sad event. It then moved to Barking remaining in service until October 1978 when it became a Barking training bus. In July 1979 it was exported to the Giraffe Bus Company in Lusaka, Zambia. **25 August 1978**

ABOVE: This was the last day that RTs worked on 'RM' route 119. RT1599 TB turns out of Hayes Road in Hayes. **25 August 1978**

BELOW: The last Friday of RT operation on route 94 finds RT1790 TB at the Petts Wood station terminus. It then moved to Barking and operated until the end in April 1979. This bus is still in use with Memory Lane. **25 August 1978**

ABOVE: RT1599 TB at Bromley North station on route 119 on the very last evening of RT operation on route 119. **25 August 1978**

BELOW: RT1790 TB in West Street Bromley on the last night of Catford garage RT operation on route 94. **25 August 1978**

ABOVE: RT422 TL suitably decorated for the very last RT trip to Orpington operated by Catford garage. It waits to leave Lewisham bus station for the final time on route 94 accompanied behind by an equally decorated preserved RT1702 which would go on to attend many other 'lasts' in LT service including the last Routemasters in 2005. **25 August 1978**

BELOW: With suitable wording applied by whitewash RT422 TL waits to leave Lewisham bus station for the last RT journey on route 94 to Orpington operated by Catford garage. **25 August 1978**

ABOVE: Nearside view of RT422 TL showing the wording and bunting applied. **25 August 1978**

BELOW: RT422 TL has arrived at Orpington St Andrews Drive and is about to start the last journey to its home – Catford garage. **25 August 1978**

68

ABOVE: The time is 0140 and RT422 TL has arrived back at Catford garage for the very last time on route 94. **26 August 1978**

BELOW: Flanked by a Routemaster and Fleetline RT422 TL slowly makes its way into Catford garage after completing the final RT journey from that garage on route 94. **26 August 1978**

ABOVE: RT422 has entered Catford garage for the last time and preserved RT1702 stands outside having accompanied the final journey on route 94. **26 August 1978**

BELOW: The Saturday Catford garage allocation to route 94 should have been be totally Routemaster, but RT422 TL has slipped out for one last time for the final day of RT operation on route 94. It is seen here in Queensway Petts Wood. **26 August 1978**

ABOVE: The last day of RT operation in South London. RT2146 is destined to be the last RT to run into Bromley garage on route 94. It stands at Petts Wood station behind preserved RT1702. **26 August 1978**

BELOW: RT2146 TB with suitable decoration for its scheduled last day in service in South London stands at Petts Wood station on route 94. It then became a training bus at Dalston and was sold to Wombwell in June 1979. **26 August 1978**

ABOVE: Unscheduled RT422 TL on a working that should be covered by a Routemaster speeds along Franks Wood Avenue on rou' 94 on the last day of RT operation from Bromley garage. **26 August 1978**

BELOW: Preserved RT1702 passes the same spot in Petts Wood suitably decorated to mark the ending of RT operation in South Londo■ Twenty Seven years later this preserved RT would be present at many of the 'last' Routemaster routes final days. **26 August 1978**

ABOVE: RT2146 TB working on route 94 on the last day passes along Queensway, Petts Wood. **26 August 1978**

BELOW: At the Petts Wood station terminus of route 94 preserved RT1702 suitably decorated for the occasion waits for the next service bus. Also waiting is preserved former STL162 which had been converted to become auxiliary breakdown tender 832J in 1950 and had only left LT stock in June 1978. **26 August 1978**

ABOVE: Leaving Brockley Rise on route 94 is RT2146 TB on the last day of RT operation by Bromley garage. **26 August 1978**

BELOW: The final RT journey on route 94 has been completed and the RT2146 TB enters the garage for last time. **26 August 1978**

RIGHT: Crowds of well wishers hamper entry into Bromley garage of the last scheduled South London RT, RT2146 TB as just finished the last trip on route 94. 26 August 1978

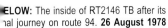

BELOW: The inside of RT2146 TB after its final journey on route 94. **26 August 1978**

LEFT: Blinds already removed and RT214□
is about to be washed after completing th□
last RT journey on route 94. **26 August 197**□

BELOW: Now how do we get that of□
Removal of the slogans on the last Sou□
London RT - 2146 TB after its final journe□
into Bromley garage. **26 August 1978**

ABOVE: It's all over for RTs in South London. Withdrawn RT4190 TB stands in the rear yard of Bromley garage, route 94 is now scheduled for Routemaster operation. This bus is still owned by members of the Barking garage Staff and Social club. **28 August 1978**

BELOW: This RF had returned to service in January 1978 and as seen here RF504 speeds under the railway bridge in Portsmouth Road on a route 218 journey. It was sold in May 1979 and sent to Guernsey; it is now back on the mainland and preserved in a gold livery and is pictured as such on page 112. **17 September 1978**

ABOVE: Seen in an empty Whale
bone Lane North RT379 BK work
route 62. Its revenue earnin
career ended in October 1978 whe
it became a training bus at Alperto
and was sold to Wombwell in Ju
1979. **24 September 1978**

LEFT: The other RT route fro
Barking – route 87 sees RT130
BK in Berwick Road Rainhan
24 September 1978

BELOW: RT2816 BK works rou
62 in Longbridge Road, it woul
stay at Barking until the end an
then move to Loughton garage an
continue there as a training bu
until withdrawal in February 197
sold to Wombwell in Marc
1979. **24 September 1978**

ABOVE: Leamington Road Harold Hill is the location for RT2517 BK working on route 87. Following the reduced requirement for RTs in October when route 87 gained RMs this RT moved to Clapton as a training bus, it was sold to Wombwell in February 1979. **24 September 1978**

RIGHT: Showing the 'missing' bonnet fleet number plate is RT3321 BK in the garage yard, despite this the bus continued in service until November 1978, the bonnet spring is attached to a hook through one of the holes normally used to attach bonnet fleet number plate. **24 September 1978**

BELOW: Withdrawn RT2797 BK stands in the front corner of the garage yard. It was sold to Wombwell in November 1978. **24 September 1978**

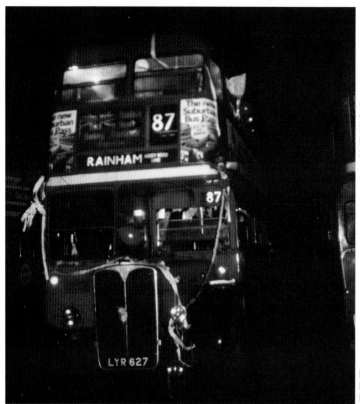

LEFT: RT3408 BK stands in Barking garage yard before making the last Mon-Fri scheduled RT journey on route 87, it then became a training bus at Bow before sale to Wombwell in May 1979. **27 October 1978**

BELOW: Ribbons adorn RT3408 BK as it waits in Barking garage yard to make the last scheduled Mon-Fri RT journey on route 87. **27 October 1978**

LEFT: RT3408 BK has just completed the last scheduled Mon-Fri journey on route 87 and its destination blinds have already been removed by garage staff. **28 October 1978**

BELOW: Kingston garage and bus station is the well known location for this view of RF471 waiting to depart on route 218. This RF had been one of two buses acting as andeigate staff buses between 1973 and 1976, returned toservice at Kingston in October 1977. After the end of RF operation it was sold to Booth's for scrap in December 1979 having failed to find a buyer via British Car Auctions. **18 March 1979**

LEFT: Turning into the BAC works at Weybridge on route 219 we find RF441. Also sold to Booth's for scrap in December 1979 having failed to find a buyer via BCA. **18 March 1979**

ABOVE: RF441 is parked at the terminus of route 219 inside the BAC works at Weybridge. **18 March 1979**

RIGHT: RF441 inside the BAC works at Weybridge on route 219. **18 March 1979**

BELOW: The terminus of route 218 was Bridge Street Staines. Here RF428 lays over. Sold to Booth's in December 1979 with RFs441 and 479. **18 March 1979**

ABOVE: RF369 seen on route 219 inside the BAC works at Weybridge. Another bus sold to Booth's in December 1979. **25 March 1979**

BELOW: Leaving the BAC Weybridge works on route 219 is RF369. **25 March 1979**

ABOVE: Shepperton station finds RF481 on route 218. Also sold to Booth's in December 1979. **25 March 1979**

BELOW: RF505 stands at Bridge Street Staines the terminus for route 218. This bus was sold for intended preservation in June 1979, but it was cut-up for spares in 1985. **25 March 1979**

ABOVE: Enthusiasts surround RF369 as it waits to depart on route 219 from Kingston bus station. **25 March 1979**

BELOW: Blinded for routes 216 and 218 we find RFs 522 and 520 K in Kingston Bus station on the last day of scheduled RF operation. RF520 was sent to Booth's for scrap in December 1979, RF522 was sold for preservation in July 1979 but has since been dismantled for spares. **30 March 1979**

ABOVE: RF502 works on route 219 in Eden Street Kingston on the last day of scheduled RF operation. Also sold to Booth's for scrap in December 1979 having failed to find a buyer via BCA. **30 March 1979**

LEFT: RF471 on the last day of scheduled RF operation at Walton station on route 218. **30 March 1979**

BELOW: Walton station is also the location of RF428 working route 218 on the last day of scheduled RF operation. **30 March 1979**

TOP: RF369 turns near Shepperton while working route 218 on the last day of scheduled RF operation. **30 March 1979**

ABOVE: RF471 on route 219 at Weybridge station on the last day of scheduled RF operation. **30 March 1979**

RIGHT: RF369 on route 219 in Weybridge on the last day of scheduled RF operation. **30 March 1979**

ABOVE: RF437 on route 218 outside Rydens school on the last day of scheduled RF operation. Also failed to find a buyer with BCA and went to Booth's for scrap in December 1979. **30 March 1979**

LEFT: RF522 on an unscheduled journey on route 216 in Kingston town centre being pursed by a Leyland National on the last day of scheduled RF operation. **30 March 1979**

BELOW: RF381 on route 219 in Kingston town centre on the last day of scheduled RF operation. **30 March 1979**

LEFT: RF502 has performed its last journey and its blinds have already been removed when seen inside Kingston garage on the last day of scheduled RF operation. **30 March 1979**

BELOW: RF507 has gained a cream band. It stands at Weybridge station for its last time on route 219 on the last day of scheduled RF operation. It was sold for preservation in June 1979 and remains thus today. **30 March 1979**

BOTTOM: RF507 would perform the very last RF journey and it carries a notice about this on its front dome on the last day of scheduled RF operation. **30 March 1979**

LEFT: En route to Staines for the las time RF507 is seen at Shepperton or route 218 on the last day of schedulec RF operation. **30 March 1979**

CENTRE LEFT: RF314 was one of extra RFs put out to bring back passen gers unable to ride aboard the last sched uled service, it waits at Staines for the last journey on the last day of schedule RF operation. **30 March 1979**

BELOW LEFT: RF507 has arrived a the Staines terminus of route 218 for th very last time on a scheduled journey **30 March 1979**

BELOW CENTRE: Clean-up work i needed inside RF507 which has jus completed the last scheduled RF jour ney. **31 March 1979**

RIGHT: Two of the three 'duplicates' RFs 492 & 511 arriving in Kingston on the last journey from Staines. RF492 was sold for preservation in in June 1979, but scrapped by PVS in 1996. RF511 was more fortunate since although it went to Wombwell in February 1980 it was saved, but is now rarely seen having been in storage since 1991. **30 March 1979**

CENTRE RIGHT: It is 0040 and the last scheduled RF journey arrives back at Kingston garage. RF507 performs this duty. **1 March 1979**

BELOW RIGHT: Crowds alongside the last RF in LT scheduled service, RF507 stands in Kingston garage after the last run. **1 March 1979**

ABOVE: It is the last Sunday of RT operation and RT1798 is at Hainault station on route 62. Although sold to Wombwell in June 1979 i was saved and still exists today in preservation. **1 April 1979**

BELOW: Green paint on the bonnet shows that this bus returned from LCBS, RT3254 is seen at Barkingside Fulwell Cross on route 62 In May 1979 this was sold to Wombwell, but after 4 years in their yard it was bought for preservation and today it is one of only three existing RTs that ran in Green Line livery and is preserved in those colours.**1 April 1979**

ABOVE: Pictured earlier working from Bromley RT1790 on the last Sunday of RT operation on route 62 at Barking Rose Lane estate. **April 1979**

BELOW: Chadwell Heath railway bridge which caused route 62 to be the last route with RTs sees RT1989 working on the last Sunday of RT operation. This bus was sold to Wombwell in June 1979. **1 April 1979**

ABOVE: The Barking town centre terminus of route 62 sees RT1301. This bus was sold for non PSV use in May 1979 and in December 1979 was exported to USA. **1 April 1979**

BELOW: The last Sunday that Barking East Street will see RTs finds RT1790 on route 62. **1 April 1979**

LEFT: Inside Barking garage awaiting the last RT journey to Creekmouth Power station and RT2541 is being prepared for the trip with suitable notices explaining this fact. This RT would take part in the final cavalcade the following weekend and was subsequently exported to Double Deck Tours, Niagara Falls, Canada, incorrectly carrying the registration plates of RT 4633, NXP 886, It was later converted into Friar Tuck's fish & chips restaurant. **1 April 1979**

BELOW: Creekmouth Power station and the last RT to this location is RT2541 – can you recognise anyone in this shot? **1 April 1979**

Still showing Creekmouth Power station in the destination display RT2541 waits to depart for the final RT journey from this location. **1 April 1979**

ABOVE: Crowds stand in front of RT2541 to record the last RT to depart from Creekmouth Power station. **1 April 1979**

RIGHT: RT2541 has just completed the last RT journey from Creekmouth Power station and stands here at the terminus in Barkingside. **1 April 1979**

BELOW: The last day of RT operation and RT624 is seen at Barking Gascoigne estate, later this day it will become the last scheduled RT with LT on route 62 and is today preserved in the heritage fleet of Ensignbus. **7 April 1979**

ABOVE: Barking Gascoigne estate and RT624 stands behind RM350 which has already displaced an RT from route 62. **7 April 1979**

BELOW: RT2240 approaches Chadwell Heath in Valence Avenue on the last morning of RT operation. This bus was in preservation from August 1979, but was one of four RTs rebuilt into two triple deckers for the Harry Potter film 'The Prisoner of Azkaban'. **7 April 1979**

ABOVE: This is the very last scheduled RT working. RT624 seen in Becontree Green Lane which is the new routeing introduced to facilitat
Routemaster operation. **7 April 1979**

BELOW: Waiting to depart from Barkingside on the last scheduled RT journey is RT624 on route 62. **7 April 1979**

ABOVE: Crowds try to get aboard RT624 as it waits to make the last scheduled RT journey from Barkingside. **7 April 1979**

BELOW: RT624 pulls away from Barkingside on route 62 making the very last scheduled RT journey. **7 April 1979**

ABOVE: The last RT arrives back at Barking garage on the last scheduled journey. RT624 has its headlights on to mark the occasion a it arrives. **7 April 1979**

BELOW: An LT traffic car and police escort lead RT624 as it makes its way towards Barking garage at the end of the last scheduled R journey. **7 April 1979**

ABOVE: Enthusiasts capture the historic moment that RT624 enters Barking garage having just completed the final scheduled journey of an RT (with running number BK 228). **7 April 1979**

BELOW: RT624 edges into Barking garage after the final RT scheduled journey on route 62. **7 April 1979**

ABOVE: Inside Barking garage as RT 624 enters for the last time after a public RT journey in London. **7 April 1979**

BELOW: RT624 inside Barking garage after the final scheduled run on route 62. **7 April 1979**

ABOVE: Still surrounded by enthusiasts RT624 seen inside Barking garage. **7 April 1979**

BELOW: Inside Barking garage we see RT2240 and two other RTs: 4633 and 2541 being prepared for the final cavalcade that afternoon. **7 April 1979**

ABOVE: RTs 1798 and 2671 inside Barking garage awaiting to perform on the final cavalcade. They will be the fourth and third buses the run. **7 April 1979**

BELOW: The fifth bus in the cavalcade would be RT3251 seen here inside Barking garage. **7 April 1979**

ABOVE: Semi-preserved RT1396 from Shaftesbury & District had made the trip to Barking for the last day and is seen here parked opposite Barking garage. **7 April 1979**

BELOW: The RTs forming the cavalcade lined up in South Park Drive before departure. Here the second bus in the run is RT4633. **7 April 1979**

ABOVE: All RTs operating the final days on route 62 carried these posters inside to explain the event. This poster is inside RT2671. **7 April 1979**

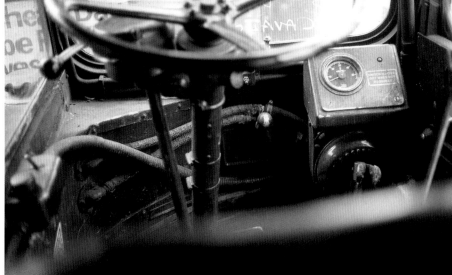

RIGHT: The cab of RT2671 destined to be the 3rd bus in the cavalcade. Chalk writing explaining this can be seen on the windscreen. This is the bus on which I travelled. **7 April 1979**

RIGHT: View of the final RT cavalcade from RT2671 the third bus which had to be pushed up Romford Road Hainault when it was unable to engage first gear and the hill proved too much for a fully laden bus in second gear. **7 April 1979**

ABOVE: The cavalcade was led by the recently restored RT1 body and here it leads the line outside Barking Town Hall. The order of vehicles was: RT1, 2541, 4633, 2671, 1798, 3251 and 624 again last. **7 April 1979**

BELOW: Offside view of the cavalcade outside Barking Town Hall. **7 April 1979**

ABOVE: Outside Barking Town Hall and behind RT1 we have 2541, 4633 and 2671. **7 April 1979**

BELOW: Outside Barking Town Hall we have RTs 2671, 1798, 3251 and 624. **7 April 1979**

Crowds greet the arrival of the cavalcade back at Barking garage in the gloom of dusk. **7 April 1979**

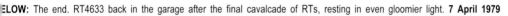

BELOW: The end. RT4633 back in the garage after the final cavalcade of RTs, resting in even gloomier light. **7 April 1979**

ABOVE: These RFs are awaiting their fate in the yard of the Wombwell Diesel Company, South Yorkshire having ben sold to them in Augu 19 77; from left to right are RFs 432, 519, 334, 617 and 513. They were all scrapped by around October 1981. **22 July 1980**

BELOW: RTs 4187, 1309, 2231 and 3351 are awaiting their fate next to the entrance of the Wombwell Diesel Company, South Yorkshir RT1309 was the only survivor being sold to The Giraffe Bus Company, Lusaka, Zambia in June 1981. **22 July 1980**

Superbly presented by Ensignbus, RT624, the very last in London Transport service, is now part of their Heritage fleet and is seen here whilst taking part in the 2007 Sidcup and Swanley running day on the former Sidcup garage operated route 161 at Chislehurst War Memorial. **8 July 2007**

Not all preserved LT vehicles are red or green. Here at the 2007 Showbus rally at the Imperial War Museum, Duxford we find RF504 preserved by Mike & Julie Betterton in a gold livery which it received while with its previous owner in autumn 2001 in recognition of the Queen's golden jubilee the following year. This bus was featured at work earlier in this book. **16 September 2007**